Mark Ziaian
World Cup 2018 Full Match Reports, 77 p + Index

Copyright 2020 Intermedia Educational Co. Ltd
ISBN 978-1-896574-06-6

Published, 2020, by Transmedia Translating and Publishing
Co., a branch of Intermedia Educational Co. Ltd, 2701-2
Forest Laneway, Toronto, Ontario, M2N 5X7.
Phone:1-647-454-0220.
Email: intermediaeducational@gmail.com
Printed and distributed by Kindle Direct Publishing,
Amazon

Cover: Mark Ziaian, image attributed to freepik.com

World Cup 2018

Full Match Reports

By Mark Ziaian

About the author

Mark Ziaian is an English journalist accredited by
FIFA and is also the inventor of the Ziaian football
rankings system at rankfootball.com.
Mark has written mostly for Score and has reported on
World Cups, the Euros, Copa America, the Asian Cup,
the Africa Cup of Nations, the Olympics,
Confederations Cups, the Premier League, the FA
Cup, women's World Cups, youth World Cups and
international friendly matches.

Table of Contents

The road to Russia 1

Russian v Saudi Arabia 5

Uruguay v Egypt 6

Iran v Morocco 7

Portugal v Spain 8

France v Australia 9

Argentina v Iceland 10

Denmark v Peru 11

Croatia v Nigeria 12

Serbia v Costa Rica 13

Mexico v Germany 14

Brazil v Switzerland 15

Sweden v South Korea 16

Belgium v Panama 17

England v Tunisia 18

Japan v Colombia 19

Senegal v Poland 20

Russia v Egypt 21

Portugal v Morocco 22

Uruguay v Saudi Arabia 23

Spain v Iran 24

Denmark v Australia 25

France v Peru 26

Croatia v Argentina 27

Brazil v Costa Rica 28

Nigeria v Iceland 29

Switzerland v Serbia 30

Belgium v Tunisia 31

Mexico v South Korea.. 32

Germany v Sweden.. 33

England v Panama 34

Japan v Senegal... 35

Colombia v Poland 36

Russia v Uruguay... 37

Saudi Arabia v Egypt 38

Portugal v Iran 39

Spain v Morocco 40

Peru v Australia... 41

France v Denmark.. 42

Argentina v Nigeria 43

Croatia v Iceland 44

Sweden v Mexico... 45

South Korea v Germany.. 46

Brazil v Serbia 47

Switzerland v Costa Rica 48

Colombia v Senegal.. 49

Poland v Japan.. 50

Belgium v England 51

Tunisia v Panama 52

GROUP TABLE AND KNOCKOUT STAGE 53

France v Argentina... 56

Uruguay v Portugal 58

Russian v Spain 59

Croatia v Denmark... 60

Brazil v Mexico.. 62

Belgium v Japan 63

Sweden v Switzerland... 65

England v Colombia 66

France v Uruguay... 68

Belgium v Brazil 69

England v Sweden.. 70

Croatia v Russia... 71

France v Belgium 73

Croatia v England... 74

Belgium v England 75

France v Croatia... 76

The road to Russia

On 2 December 2010 Russia was elected by FIFA to host the 2018 World Cup.

For the first time all 209 members of FIFA, apart from automatically qualified Russia, applied to enter the qualifying rounds. Later Gibraltar and Kosovo joined FIFA and were allowed to take part in the qualifiers. Bhutan and South Sudan also made their World Cup qualification debuts.

Indonesia were expelled from the competition due to government interference in the country's domestic league and Zimbabwe for outstanding debts to national manager José Claudinei, before playing their first matches.

Asia – The World Cup qualifiers kicked off on 12 March 2015 in Dili, with East Timor taking on Mongolia and Quito scoring the first goal of the competition after only 4 minutes for the hosts who went on to win 4-1, but were later disqualified for fielding several ineligible players. Debutants Bhutan stunned Sri Lanka 1-0 in Colombo and were among the 6 teams to join the rest of Asia in the second round where they were annihilated 15-0 in Qatar and finished bottom of their group. The best teams from the 8 groups in round 2 made up 2 groups of 6 in the final round, with the top 2 qualifying for the finals and the third teams playing each other home and away for the right to play-off against the fourth team from CONCACAF for the final spot in the World Cup.

Iran became the first team to qualify, followed by Japan, South Korea and Saudi Arabia. Australia who lost out to Saudi Arabia on direct qualification on goal difference, scraped past Syria in extra-time to reach the inter-confederation play-offs.

CONCACAF – The North, Central American and Caribbean section began on 22 March 2015 with the lowest ranked teams in the region playing a knockout round to join slightly higher ranked teams in the next rounds. In round 4, Trinidad & Tobago, Panama, Honduras, United States, Mexico and Costa Rica were awaiting the survivors from the previous rounds to form 3 groups of 4 teams and eliminate them to progress to the final group where Mexico, Costa Rica and Panama would qualify directly for the World Cup, with Honduras heading to the play-offs to meet the fifth team from Asia (Australia). The United States of America failed to reach Russia after losing 2-1 in Trinidad & Tobago.

Oceania – With no guaranteed representation in the World Cup finals from this section, the 11 members played for the chance to meet the fifth-best team from South America in a two-legged play-off to qualify for the World Cup in Russia.

The 4 lowest ranked teams in the region played one another in Tonga with Samoa winning the group ahead of American Samoa and Cook Islands on goal difference, leaving the hosts pointless.

In the second round, the Samoans were brushed aside by hosts Papua New Guinea, New Caledonia and Tahiti from group A, who were joined by New Zealand, Solomon Islands and Fiji from group B where Vanuatu were left behind.

The 6 teams were drawn into 2 groups and the group winners, New Zealand and Solomon Islands, met with New Zealand winning 8-3 on aggregate to reach the intercontinental play-offs.

Africa – After the expulsion of Zimbabwe, the names of the remaining 53 teams were placed into two pots based on their rankings. The 26 lowest ranked teams were drawn to play a home and away knockout round and the winners were added to the top pot to create 20 ties in the second round.

The 20 winners were drawn into 5 groups with the top team from each group qualifying for the 2018 World Cup. Tunisia topped their group ahead of DR Congo with only a point to spare, whereas Nigeria, Morocco, Senegal and Egypt qualified from their groups with more dominance.

South America – The 10 members made up a league with the top 4 of Brazil, Uruguay, Argentina and Colombia qualifying directly for the World Cup.

Reigning South American champions, Chile, shot themselves in the foot when they protested after a goalless draw at home to Bolivia that their visitors had fielded an ineligible player. Chile gained 2 more points when they were awarded the match 3-0 by FIFA who consequently discovered that the same player had been used in Bolivia's 2-0 home win over Peru. The match was awarded to Peru, giving them 3 extra points which proved to be crucial as they finished ahead of Chile on goal difference to reach the intercontinental play-offs against the top team from Oceania (New Zealand).

Europe – With Russia qualifying as hosts, the remaining 54 teams were drawn into 9 groups of 6 teams. The top teams from each group would qualify for the World Cup while the 8 best runners-up would enter a home and away play-off round the determine the remaining 4 qualifiers.

France, Portugal, Germany, Serbia, Poland, England, Spain, Belgium and Iceland qualified as group winners. The Germans cruised to the finals with 10 straight wins while Portugal qualified on goal difference ahead of Switzerland who joined Sweden, Northern Ireland, Republic of Ireland, Denmark, Italy, Greece and Croatia in the play-offs. The Netherlands, who won third place in the previous World Cup, finished behind Sweden and Italy in their group, failing to make it to the play-offs

Iceland became the smallest country ever to qualify for the World Cup finals.

Play offs – In the intercontinental play-offs, Australia returned from Honduras with a goalless draw to qualify with a 3-1 win in Sydney and Peru who played a goalless match in New Zealand celebrated qualification with a 2-0 victory on home soil.

In the European play-offs, there were also goalless draws in every tie. A single goal in Belfast was enough to send Switzerland through against Northern Ireland while Croatia did the damage in their 4-1 victory against Greece in Zagreb. The Republic of Ireland drew in Denmark and took an early lead in Dublin but were demolished 5-1 by the Danes with Christian Eriksen netting a hat-trick and one goal in Sweden was enough to send the Swedes through and deny Italy a place in the finals for the first time since 1958.

Group A

Russian subs sink Saudi Arabia

Russia 5 Saudi Arabia 0 (Moscow)

The 2018 World Cup began with a thumping 5-0 win for hosts Russia over Saudi Arabia.

In the 12th minute a cross from Golovin found Yuri Gazinski who picked the far corner of the net with a header to open the scoring in the tournament. With 2 minutes of the half remaining, Russia doubled their lead when substitute Denis Cheryshef picked up a pass from Golovin and left two Saudi defenders sliding to coolly drive the ball into the roof of the net.

Saudi Arabia statistically had more possession but could only create one chance when a low cross across the face of goal went begging as a sliding Alsahlawy failed to connect.

The tall Artem Dzyuba was introduced in the 70th minute and made an immediate impact as he met a cross a minute later to head in number 3 for the hosts. A minute into stoppage time, Dzyuba nodded the ball down into the path of Cheryshef who curled it brilliantly into the top corner with the outside of his left foot for his 2nd of the game and 3 minutes later Aleksandr Golovin curled a free kick round the wall and past the keeper to make it 5-0 to the hosts on the opening day.

Group A

Pharaohs fall to late goal

Uruguay 1 Egypt 0 (Ekaterinburg)

Uruguay left it late to wake up and claim 3 points against Egypt who were without their talisman Mohamed Salah.

In the 24th minute Suarez miskicked the ball into the side netting from inside the 6-yard box and a minute into the 2nd half, with only the keeper to beat, saw his effort averted by the keeper's knee. Suarez took his time and failed to get past El Shenawy in the Egypt goal in the 73rd minute and in the 83rd minute Cavani's fierce volley from just outside the box was superbly kept out by the Egyptian custodian.

Egypt had some spells of pressure, but in the 88th minute Canavi struck the post from a free kick and just before full time Jose Maria Gimenez rose highest to break Egyptian hearts with a piercing header.

Group B

Moroccan misery

Iran 1 Morocco 0 (Saint Petersburg)

An own goal in stoppage time gave Iran the edge over Morocco in Saint Petersburg.

The Iranians, who survived a scramble in front of goal in the 19th minute, had an excellent chance to score when Azmoun was free on goal but failed to shoot past Munir who got an arm to the rebound from Jahanbakhsh.

Beiranvand was at full stretch in the 80th minute to turn a crisp Ziyech volley from the edge of the area around the post and keep the match goalless, but deep into stoppage time Morocco gave away a needles free kick down the left flank which was floated into the box for Bouhaddouz to put past his keeper with a diving header and send the Iranians into delirium.

Group B

Ronaldo stars in Iberian thriller

Portugal 3 Spain 3 (Sochi)

Cristiano Ronaldo scored a hat-trick to foil a Spanish comeback as Portugal draw 3-3 with their neighbours in Sochi.

After only 3 minutes, Ronaldo went down in the box, picked himself up and sent de Gea the wrong way from the spot, but in the 24th minute Spain equalised when Diego Costa showed strength and skill to bring a long ball down outside the box elude the Portuguese defenders in the box and finish with aplomb. Two minutes later Isco's thunderous shot came off the underside of the bar, but at the other end with a minute of the half left, Ronaldo's shot was spilled into the net by de Gea and Portugal went into the break leading.

In the 55th minute, a free kick crossed into the area was headed down by Busquets and forced over the line by Costa. Three minutes later Spain went 3-2 up when a Nacho screamer went in off the base of the post, but in the 88th minute Ronaldo completed his hat-trick with a stunning free kick to level the score.

Group C

French assistance

France 2 Australia 1 (Kazan)

France overcame Australia 2-1 with the help of video technology in Kazan.

After a relatively uneventful first half, the crowd was given something to talk about in the 54th minute when Griezmann picked up a through ball and was dispossessed with a tackle just inside the box. Initially the referee allowed play to continue, but after viewing his monitor on the sideline pointed to the spot from which Griezmann smashed the ball in for the first ever VAR penalty awarded in a World Cup.

There was no need for VAR in the 61st minute when the referee awarded Australia a penalty for handball and Mile Jedinak rolled the ball past Loris.

After some good interplay in the 80th minute, Paul Pogba stretched a foot to deflect the ball past the keeper and over the line via the crossbar and France celebrated as goal-line technology confirmed the goal.

Group D

Hand of cod holds Argentina

Argentina 1 Iceland 1 (Moscow)

Hannes Halldorsson saved a Messi penalty as Iceland held Argentina to a 1-1 draw in their first ever World Cup match.

In the 19th minute Aguero received the ball in the box, turned and dispatched it into to top corner, but 4 minutes later Argentina failed to clear a low cross and Alfred Finnbogason sidefooted the leveller from 6 yards out.

Argentina were awarded a penalty in the 63rd minute, but Halldorsson dived to his right to deny Messi. The Icelandic keeper got down quickly in the 85th minute and pushed away an elusive inswinging low cross to ensure the smallest nation ever to qualify for a World Cup earned a point in their first match.

Saturday June 16th

Group C

Peru rue penalty miss

Denmark 1 Peru 0 (Saransk)

Denmark picked up 3 points after a Peruvian penalty miss in the first half in a group C match in Saransk.

In the 13th minute Carrillo curled a low ball to the far corner which Schmeichel got down to parry and just before the break Peru were awarded a penalty with the help of VAR, but Cueva skyed the ball over the bar and into the crowd.

In the 59th minute, Eriksen found Yussuf Poulsen who slotted the ball in at the near post. Two minutes later Schmeichel kept out an effort from Flores and in the 79th minute a backheel from Guerrero went agonisingly wide while in the 84th minute the Danes cleared off the line and moments later at the other end Gallese made himself big in the Peru goal to block the advancing Eriksen's effort with his shoulder.

Group D

Croatia comfortable

Croatia 2 Nigeria 0 (Kaliningrad)

An own goal and a penalty gave Croatia a 2-0 win over a disappointing Nigeria in Kaliningrad.

A corner in the 32nd minute was headed onto the diving head of Mandzukic and in off a Nigerian player to open the scoring for Croatia who should have doubled their lead in the 56th minute when Rebic ran onto a cross but missed the target from close range.

Luka Modric found the bottom left corner of the net from the penalty spot in the 70th minute with the keeper moving in the wrong direction and Croatia were home and dry.

Group E

Serbia on target

Serbia 1 Costa Rica 0 (Samara)

A single goal gave Serbia a winning start as they defeated Costa Rica in Samara.

A Gonzalez free header for Costa Rica flew over the bar in the 12th minute and 5 minutes into the second half Mitrovic was through on goal but couldn't knock the ball past Navas. Six minutes later Navas was beaten when Serbia's skipper, Aleksandar Kolarov, struck a peach of a free kick beyond his reach. In the 76th minute Kostic miscued a low cross in front of goal but one goal was enough to give Serbia the points.

Group F

Mexico champion beaters

Mexico 1 Germany 0 (Moscow)

Defending champions Germany began their World Cup campaign with a defeat to Mexico in Moscow.

The Mexicans started the match on the front foot and within minutes the German defence had to make a crucial block to intercept a shot in the box. Neuer had to get down to stop a shot in the 10th minute and a header 4 minutes later.

In the 35th minute, Mexico broke through with Hernandez feeding Lozano who cut back inside and beat Neuer at the near post. Three minutes later, a free kick from Kroos was tipped onto the bar.

In the second half the Germans push forward while the Mexicans were wasteful on the counter. In the 89th minute a desperate shot from Brandt struck the outside of the upright and Mexico held on to secure a famous victory over the Germans.

Group E

Zuber Swiss draw with Brazil

Brazil 1 Switzerland 1 (Rostov on Don)

Out to put the ghost of 2014 to rest, Brazil found Switzerland a hard nut to crack.

In the 11th minute the ball reached Paulinho who scuffed his shot in front of goal, but in the 20th minute Philippe Coutinho curled the ball brilliantly into the far top corner off the post to give Brazil the lead.

In the 50th minute, a corner-kick was delivered onto the head of Steven Zuber in front of goal and the Swiss were level. A powerful header from Neymar in the 88th minute was straight at Sommer who had to dive to his right 2 minutes later to keep out a header from Firmino, while a snapshot from Miranda in stoppage time bounced past the post as Switzerland held on to claim a 1-1 draw with Brazil.

Monday June 18ᵗʰ

Group F

Swedish sweet spot

Sweden 1 South Korea 0 (Nizhny Novgorod)

A VAR penalty helped Sweden get the better of South Korea and pick up 3 vital points.

Cho Hyun-Woo made a point blank save to deny Berg's sidefooter from 6 yards out in the 20th minute and got down to block a header from Jansson in the 56th minute but in the 64th minute, after video assistance, the referee pointed to the spot and Swedish captain Andreas Granqvist sent the Korean keeper the wrong way to give Sweden a win in their opening match.

Group G

Lukaku double boosts Belgium

Belgium 3 Panama 0 (Sochi)

A second-half brace from Romelu Lukaku helped Belgium to a 3-0 win over Panama in Sochi.

The Panamanians held Belgium to a goalless first half with a crucial interception in front of goal by Torres in the 21st minute and a save from Penedo as Hazard ran into the box and whacked the ball towards the near post, but 2 minutes into the second half the ball fell to Dries Mertens whose dipping volley from the corner of the box broke the deadlock.

In the 54th minute Carrasco got behind the Belgian defence but was blocked by Courtois and in the 69th minute Lukaku dived to head de Bruyne's delightful cross into the back of the net. In the 75th minute, Hazard ran into the Panama half and threaded the ball to Lukaku who dinked the keeper for the third.

Group G

Tunisia double-Kaned

England 2 Tunisia 1 (Volgogrod)

Harry Kane scored twice as England left it late to dispose of Tunisia.

England got off to an explosive start and after a swift attack in the 5th minute, Lingard's sidefooter from 6 yards out was denied by the trailing foot of Hassen in the Tunisia goal. In the 11th minute Hassen majestically kept out Stone's firm header but Harry Kane was on hand to open the scoring for England.

Ben Mustapha replaced the injured Hassen and had to get down to hold onto a crisp Henderson volley form 25 yards out in the 18th minute. England were unable to convert their chances and in the 33rd minute when Tunisia were awarded a soft penalty, Ferjani Sassi dispatched the ball into the corner of the net past the diving Pickford.

A minute before the break, Lingard poked a long ball past the onrushing keeper but his effort hit the wrong side of the post. After the break, Tunisia played with more belief, but England didn't give up and in stoppage time a corner kick was knocked on for Kane to stoop and head in the winner at the far post.

Group H

Japanese mountain too steep

Japan 2 Colombia 1 (Saransk)

Reduced to 10 men and a goal down early on in the match, Colombia fought back but ended up losing their match to Japan.

In the 3rd minute Osaka raced towards goal only to see his effort blocked by Ospina, but the return from Kagawa was handled by Sanchez who was shown the first red card of this World Cup. Shinji Kagawa rolled the ball past the deceived Ospina from the spot to leave the 10 Colombians with a daunting task ahead of them.

In the 39th minute, a Quintero free kick went under the jumping Japanese wall and Kawashima couldn't prevent the ball from crossing the line. Ospina got down to save from Osako at his near post in the 54th minute and dived to his left to keep out a curler from Inui 3 minutes later, but was beaten in the 73rd minute when Osaka got up to flick his header in off the post from a corner kick. James Rodrigues had a chance late on for Colombia but blasted high.

Group H

Senegal enjoy Polish gifts

Senegal 2 Poland 1 (Moscow)

An own goal and a defensive error helped Senegal to a victory over Poland.

In the 37th minute, Gueye's shot from outside the area was deflected past Szczensy for an own goal. N'Diaye dived to punch away a free kick from Lewandowski in the 50th minute, but on the hour-mark Krychowiak lofted the ball back into his own half and Niang stole it from the outcoming Szczensy to conquer the empty net and double Senegal's lead.

In the 70th minute Milik flicked the ball past the post from close range and in the 86th minutes a free kick was floated into the box and headed home by Krychowiak, but it was too little too late for Poland.

Tuesday June 19th

Group A

On the brink

Russia 3 Egypt 1 (St Petersburg)

A 3-1 win for Russia over Egypt puts the hosts on the brink of qualification for the next round while the Pharaohs are left hanging by a thread.

The closest either side came in the first half was when Trezeguet curled the ball inches wide of the post in the 16th minute, but 2 minutes into the second half Russia took the lead when Zobnin's mis-hit shot went in off an Egyptian knee for an own goal.

In the 59th minute, Fernandez pulled the ball back from the byline for Denis Cherychef to sidefoot past El Shenaway and 3 minutes later a long ball to the edge of the area was chested down by Dzyuba who poked it past a defender and scored with an accurate finish. In the 72nd minute, the referee awarded a free kick just outside the box but with the help of VAR changed it to a penalty which Mohamed Salah dispatched with aplomb.

Group B

Ronaldo sends Morocco home

Portugal 1 Morocco 0 (Moscow)

An early goal by Cristiano Ronaldo sealed Morocco's fate as they suffered their second 1-0 defeat in a row.

Ronaldo lost his marker and flung himself to head in a cross in the 4th minute while at the other end in the 11th minute the Portuguese keeper got down on the line to hold a header from Da Costa. In the 39th minute Ronaldo lifted the ball over the Moroccan backline for Guedes to shoot but El Kajoui stood firm and saved with one hand.

Belhanda's powerful shot in the 56th minute was too close to Patricio who a minute later made a magnificent save to keep out an awkward header from the same player. Morocco had plenty of possession but their determination to succeed was not matched by their finishing skill.

Group A

Suarez goal settles group

Uruguay 1 Saudi Arabia 0 (Rostov on Don)

A single goal for Uruguay against Saudi Arabia was enough to see them though with hosts Russia while Saudi Arabia and Egypt were eliminated.

A corner in the 23rd minute was turned in by Luis Suarez from 6 yards out for the only goal of the match. Muslera tipped a shot from Hatan over the bar in the 26th minute and 3 minutes later the same player got on the end of a cross but hit the ball into the crowd.

Al-Owais got down to punch away a free kick from Suarez in the 51st minute and in the 62nd minute saw Cavani's beautifully weighted cross fly over the bar from a Sanchez diving header on the 6-yard line. With 4 minutes to go, Cavani ran into the box, but his shot on the turn was blocked by the Saudi keeper.

Group B

Spain breach Iranian defence

Spain 1 Iran 0 (Kazan)

An Iranian side hell-bent on not conceding, lost 1-0 to Spain in Kazan.

The Iranians defended tooth and claw and didn't let the Spaniards get anywhere near their goal in the first half. In the 49th minute, Beiranvand clumsily saved a shot from Vazquez but did well to knock the loose ball out for a corner. A throw-in for Iran in the 53rd was knocked down in the box but Ansarifard's fierce volley hit the wrong side of the net and a minute later Diego Costa turned in the box allowing a defensive toe-poke to ricochet off him and past Beiranvand to break the deadlock.

Iran came out of their shells after the goal and had a goal disallowed by VAR for offside in the 62nd minute. In the 70th minute, a low corner-kick was cut back and resulted in a scramble on the Iran goal-line, but with 8 minutes remaining Iran came close to levelling the score when Amiri nutmegged Pique and delivered a cross, but Taremi headed over from inside the 6-yard box.

Group C

Video keeps Oz alive

Denmark 1 Australia 1 (Samara)

Australia converted a video-assisted penalty to draw 1-1 with Denmark and keep their World Cup hopes alive.

Denmark took an early lead when Jorgensen skilfully knocked the ball on for Christian Eriksen to slam in with a rising volley from inside the area in the 7th minute, but in the 37th minute the referee awarded a penalty to Australia for handball after reviewing the incident on the touchline and Mile Jedinak sent Schmeichel the wrong way with a concentrated spot kick.

In the 71st minute a rasping shot from Mooy flew over the crossbar and with 2 minutes remaining, Schmeichel beat away Arzani's angled shot towards the far post and clawed out Leckie's effort from the top corner.

Group C

Peru fall short

France 1 Peru 0 (Ekaterinburg)

France are through to the next round after a 1-0 win over Peru that ends the South American team's hopes of progress in the World Cup.

A daisy-cutter on the volley from Griezmann was blocked by the knees of the keeper in the 16th minute and in the 31st minute Guerrero touched the ball past a defender in the box, but his shot was blocked by Lloris. Three minutes later, an attempt from Giroud was deflected over Gallese for Kylian Mbappe to tap over the line and 2 minutes before the break, after some good football by France, Gallese put his hands up to stop a Hernandez shot from the left. Aquino let fly in the 50th minute but his swerving shot came off the angle of the woodwork and with Peru creating no more chances their fate was sealed.

Thursday June 21st

Group D

Croatia rattle Argentina

Croatia 3 Argentina 0 (Nizhny Novgorod)

A goalkeeping howler by Argentina's Willy Caballero opened the door to Croatia who took full advantage of their South American opponent's frailties.

In the 5th minute, a shot across goal by Perisic was touched away for a corner while on the half hour-mark Argentina came close when after a defensive mix-up the ball fell to Perez who with the goal gaping couldn't hit the target; and 3 minutes later, at the other end Mandzukic dived to put a free header wide from Inside the 6-yard box.

In the 53rd minute, Calallero sliced a back-pass into the air and Ante Rebic volleyed over him leaving the keeper with egg on his face and Croatia a goal up. In the 64th minute Higuain cut the ball back for Meza to shoot but his effort was blocked on the line by Subasic and 2 minutes later Mandzukic hit the side netting for Croatia.With 10 minutes to go, Luka Modric curled to ball past the diving Caballero from 25 yards out and in the 87th minute Rakitic curled a free kick onto the crossbar. In stoppage time Croatia broke through and Caballero saved a shot from Rakitic but Kovacic picked up the rebound and squared it back to Rakitic who rolled in the 3rd for Croatia.

Friday June 22nd

Group E

Brazil need time

Brazil 2 Costa Rica 0 (St Petersburg)

Costa Rica shut shop for 90 minutes against Brazil but went out after conceding 2 goals in stoppage time.

Gamboa ran to the byline in the 13th minute and pulled the ball back for Borgos who rolled it past the Brazil post. At the other end in the 27th minute Neymar ran into the box but saw his effort foiled by Navas.

Four minutes into the second half, Jesus nodded the ball onto the bar and Coutinho's shot from the follow up was deflected wide. In the 56th minute Paulinho cut the ball back to Neymar, whose shot was tipped over the bar by Navas while 3 minutes later Paulinho's shot was too close to the keeper and in the 72nd minute Neymar curled the ball just wide of the upright.

In the 78th minute, Neymar went down in the box and the referee awarded a penalty only to change his mind after help from VAR. In stoppage time Coutinho ran onto a knockdown from Firmino to knock the ball past Navas. Brazil found time for another goal when Douglas Costa received the ball in the box and passed it across goal past the diving Navas for Neymar to knock into the empty net.

Group D

Musa double melts Iceland

Nigeria 2 Iceland 0 (Volgograd)

Ahmed Musa scored twice, and Iceland missed a penalty as Nigeria celebrated a win in Volgograd.

Iceland started well and Gylfi Sigurdsson saw his free kick tipped over in the 3rd minute but 4 minutes after the break Moses ran down the right and crossed the ball to Musa who brought it down with his right foot and smashed it past the keeper into the roof of the net.

Ndidi's dipping shot in the 57th minute was palmed over the bar and in the 74th minute Musa's swerving shot hit the bar, but a minute later he ran into the area, got away from the keeper and fired past two defenders on the line to double his tally. With 10 minutes remaining Iceland were awarded a video assisted penalty but Gylfi Sigurdsson cleared the crossbar.

Friday June 22nd

Group E

Swiss turnaround

Switzerland 2 Serbia 1 (Kaliningrad)

Switzerland came from behind against Serbia with a late winner to turn the table on the Serbs.

With a win securing a place in the next round, Serbia began on the front foot and in the 5th minute Sommer got down to his left to save a header from Mitrovic, but moments later Mitrovic beat the Swiss keeper with a glancing header high into the net. In the 29th minute, Zuber fed the ball to Seferovic but Stojkovic in the Serbia goal saved his close-range effort.

A blocked shot in the 52nd minute fell to Granit Xhaka who smacked in a swerving ball from outside the box to level the score while 6 minutes later Shaqiri curled a superb ball from the corner of the box onto the far angle of the woodwork. In the 90th minute, Xherdan Shaqiri raced from the halfway line to slide the ball past the keeper and win the match for the Swiss.

Group G

Five-star Belgium

Belgium 5 Tunisia 2 (Moscow)

Romelu Lukaku and Eden Hazard scored 2 apiece as Belgium outclassed Tunisia 5-2 in Moscow.

It took Belgium 5 minutes to open the scoring when Hazard rolled the ball in from the penalty spot past the stationary Ben Mustapha, and in the 16th minute Mertens passed the ball to Lukaku in space who found the corner of the net from the edge the box. Two minutes later, a free kick from the left edge of the area was delivered by Khazri onto the head of Dylan Bronn who reduced the deficit for Tunisia, but Meunier played a through ball to Lukaku who dinked the keeper with the last kick of the half.

Six minutes into the second-half, Hazard got on the end of a long ball and knocked it past the keeper to make it 4 for Belgium. Substitute Batshuayi rounded the keeper in the 76th minute but saw his effort cleared off the line, and 3 minutes later with the goal at his mercy he hit the underside of the bar from a few yard out, but having hit a powerful volley straight at the keeper from 6 yards out in the 81st minute he slid onto a cross in the 90th minute to steer the ball past the keeper for Belgium's fifth. Tunisia scored a consolation goal in the last minute of stoppage time when Khazri got enough on a cutback from Nagguez to see the ball creep past Courtois.

Group F

Mexico win again

Mexico 2 South Korea 1 (Rostov-on-Don)

A 2-1 victory for Mexico over South Korea made it 2 wins out of 2 for the Mexicans.

In the 22nd minute, Son had 2 powerful shots blocked and Ki's header from the ensuing corner-kick was tipped over the bar, but 2 minutes later a sliding tackle in the box resulted in a handball and Carlos Vela sent Cho the wrong way from the spot.

In the 58th minute, Guardado got a shot in from just inside the box, but Cho flew to his right to keep it out of the top corner and in the 66th minute Lozano ran into the Korean half and fed Javier Hernandez who left a defender on the floor to slot the ball past Cho.

The South Koreans scored a consolation goal in stoppage time when Son Heung-Min cut in from the right and unleashed a screamer past the diving Ochoa, but it was too little too late for the Koreans.

Saturday June 23rd

Group F

Back from the dead

Germany 2 Sweden 1 (Sochi)

Germany came from behind to defeat Sweden deep into stoppage time and keep their hopes alive.

Knowing that a defeat would see them eliminated, the Germans showed hunger from the start and peppered the Swedish goal, but in the 12th minute Berg ran on goal and was overpowered in the box, sparking unsuccessful claims for a penalty. Sweden took the lead in the 32nd minute when Ola Toivonen received the ball between 2 Germans and lifted it over the keeper. In the 39th minute, Olsen saved from a deflected shot and kept out the follow up, but on the stroke of half-time it was Neuer who was brought into action when he saved from a Berg header.

Three minutes into the second-half Germany drew level when Marco Reus knocked a ball from the left in with the side of his knee, but in the 82nd minute Germany were reduced to 10 men when Boateng was sent off for a second yellow. In the 88th minute Olsen made a point-blank save when he punched a header from Gomez over the bar and in stoppage time a piledriver from Brandt came off the post, but 5 minutes into added-on time, a free kick from the left side of the box was curled brilliantly by Toni Kroos into the far top corner past the despairing Olsen for the German winner.

Sunday June 24th

Group G

England cruise past Panama

England 6 Panama 1 (Nizhny Novgorod)

Harry Kane scored a hat-trick as England pummelled Panama 6-1 to reach the next round.

John Stones opened the scoring in the 8th minute with a thumping header into the bottom corner of the net from a corner-kick and Kane doubled England's lead in the 20th minute, scoring emphatically from the penalty spot. Jesse Lingard picked the top corner with a beautifully stuck ball from outside the box in the 36th minute and 4 minutes later a cleverly-taken free kick was headed to Stirling whose header was saved by the keeper but nodded in by Stones. Kane smashed in another penalty just before the break after some wrestling in the box to make it 5-0 at half time.

England took it easy in the second half and scored their 6th in the 62nd minute when a shot from Loftus-Cheek took a deflection off Kane for his hat-trick, but it was Panama who had the last laugh when Felipe Baloy slid onto a cross from a free kick to knock the ball past Pickford and register Panama's first ever World Cup goal.

Sunday June 24th

Group H

Honours even

Japan 2 Senegal 2 (Ekaterinburg)

Japan and Senegal shared the points in a 2-2 draw at the top of the table in group H.

In the 11th minute Japan failed to head a cross away and a low shot was punched by Kawashima and deflected in off the leg of Sadio Mane, but in the 35th minute Takashi Inui picked up Nagatomo's ball in the box, opened his body and sent it to the far corner of the net.

In the 64th minute, Osako ran onto a long ball and backheeled it into the box for Inui to stroke onto the crossbar, but in the 71st minute Senegal retook the lead when Moussa Wague ran onto a ball played across goal and knocked it into the roof of the net. Japan equalised 7 minutes later when the Senegalese keeper failed to claim a high ball into the box and Takashi pulled the ball back from the by-line for substitute Keisuke Honda to score and become Asia's top scorer in World Cup history.

Sunday June 24th

Group H

Poland crash out

Colombia 3 Poland 0 (Kazan)

Colombia bounced back from their defeat against Japan with a convincing 3-0 victory over Poland.

After a lot of running by both sides, Colombia took control in the 40th minute when Rodriguez lifted the ball into the 6-yard box for the towering Yerry Mina to head in.

A long ball in the 58th minute reached Lewandowsky, but Colombian keeper Ospina bravely got in his way, and in the 70th minute Colombia went further ahead when Quintero passed the ball to Rademel Falcoa who confidently stroked it past Szczesny with the outside of his right foot. Five minute later Guardado received the ball in acres of space and went on to place it past the keeper. There was no consolation for Poland as a thunderous shot by Lewandowski was tipped over the bar in the last minute.

Monday June 25th

Group A

Russia brought down to earth

Russia 0 Uruguay 3 (Samara)

Uruguay won the group after an easy 3-0 win over hosts Russia.

In the 10th minute Luis Suarez fired a free kick into the bottom right corner and in the 23rd minute a corner was cleared out of the area as far as Stuani whose shot was deflected past the Russian keeper.

Russia were reduced to 10 men when Smolnikov was dismissed for his second yellow card offence 9 minutes before the break. The Russians held on until the last minute of the match when Akifneev saved a header from a corner kick and Cavani knocked in the rebound. Russia go through as runners up in the group.

Group A

Saudis salvage some pride

Saudi Arabia 2 Egypt 1 (Volgograd)

Saudi Arabia came from behind against Egypt to score a late winner and go home happy.

Mohamed Salah got on the end of a long pass from Abdalla Said and lifted the ball over the keeper to put Egypt into the lead in the 22nd minute, and 2 minutes later Salah received another through ball, but with only the keeper to beat, chipped it wide of the post. In the 39th minute, the referee awarded Saudi Arabia a penalty for handball and the Egyptian keeper El Hadary, the oldest player in the history of the World Cup, did brilliantly to get down and push Fahad's spot kick onto the bar, but in first-half stoppage-time Saudi Arabia got another chance from the spot and this time Salman Al Faraj sent the keeper the wrong way.

El Hadary tipped Almoqahwi's firm header over the bar in the 70th minute, but late in stoppage time the ball was played into the box from the right and Salem El Dossari scored the winner with a low shot across goal.

Group B

VAR scare for Portugal

Portugal 1 Iran 1 (Saransk)

Portugal could have been eliminated but had to settle for second spot in the group and a meeting with Uruguay after a 1-1 draw with Iran in a match that was littered with controversial VAR decisions.

With the teams ready to go into the break at 0-0, Ricardo Quaresma played a quick one-two before curling the ball with the outside of his right boot into the far corner beyond the reach of Beiranvand. The Iranian keeper became a hero when he dived to his left to save a penalty from Ronaldo after the referee had awarded Portugal a soft penalty with the help of VAR in the 51st minute.

In stoppage time the referee once again turned to VAR to overturn his initial decision and awarded Iran an even softer penalty which Karim Ansarifard dispatched confidently into the top corner. Moments later Portugal faced elimination but Taremi could only hit the side-netting from the edge of the 6-yard box.

Monday June 25th

Group B

Morocco stretch Spain

Spain 2 Morocco 2 (Kaliningrad)

Spain needed a goal in stoppage time to earn a 2-2 draw with Morocco and top the group.

A Spanish mix-up on the centre-line in the 14th minute allowed Khalid Boutaib to steal the ball and run towards goal before slotting it past de Gea, but 5 minutes later the Spaniards passed the ball into the box and Iniesta pulled the ball back for Isco to smash into the roof of the net. Boutaib was once again set free to run at goal in the 25th minute, but de Gea got in his way at the near post.

Ten minutes into the second half, an Amrabat screamer struck the underside of the top corner with de Gea a mere admirer. In the 62nd minute Isco's towering header was cleared off the line by Saiss, but in the 81st minute, at the other end Youssef En Nesyri met a corner kick with a bullet header to put Morocco back in the lead. In stoppage time, a quickly-taken corner was crossed into the 6-yard area for Iago Aspas to flick in and give Spain a draw.

Tuesday June 26th

Group C

Peru send Aussies down under

Peru 2 Australia 0 (Sochi)

Australia finished bottom of their group after losing 2-0 to Peru.

In the 18th minute, Cueva got into the box from the left and lifted the ball to Andre Carillo who drilled his volley past Ryan in the Australia goal. Rogic had a chance for Australia in the 27th minute when he weaved his way into the box, but his effort was blocked by the keeper.

Five minutes into the second-half, Paolo Guerrero got a foot to the ball in the box to volley in number 2 for Peru with the help of a deflection.

Tuesday June 26th

Group C

Top bores

France 0 Denmark 0 (Moscow)

In the top-of-the-table clash France and Denmark played out the first goalless match of this World Cup.

Neither side showed much interest in changing the result with the French sitting at the top and the Danes harbouring no ambitions to top the group.

Having introduced fresh legs, the French strode forward in the last 10 minutes and Schmeichel turned away a low curler from Fakir in the 82nd minute, but on the final whistle the teams left the pitch to the echo of boos from the crowd ringing in their ears.

Group D

Late joy for Argentina

Argentina 2 Nigeria 1 (St Petersburg)

Needing a win to avoid elimination at the group stage, Argentina scored a late winner against Nigeria to go through at the African side's expense.

A long ball in the 14th minute found Messi who controlled it with two touches on the run and rifled it into the far corner of the net. In the 27th minute Uzoho acted quickly to foil a through ball to Higuaín and in the 34th minute a Messi free kick came off the post.

Four minutes after the break, Nigeria were awarded a penalty for holding in the box and Victor Moses rolled the ball in to give the Africans parity and in the 75th minute the ball fell invitingly to Ighalo who could only volley wide from 10 yards out.

With time running out for Argentina, Mercado put in a cross in the 86th minute and Marcos Rojo placed his volley into the bottom right corner to give Argentina life and send Nigeria home.

Group D

Croatia end Icelandic dream

Croatia 2 Iceland 1 (Rostov-on-Don)

Iceland's hope of reaching the next round ended with a 2-1 defeat to Croatia who finish with a 100% winning record.

The closest either side came in the first half was in stoppage time when Kalinic parried a shot from Gunnarsson that was heading for the top corner, but in the 52nd minute Milan Badelj hit the Iceland crossbar from distance and a minute later ran onto a ball in the box bouncing it with a half-volley into the net. Two minutes after conceding the goal, following a long throw-in, Ingason's header was tipped over by Kalinic and moments later the same player headed onto the top of the crossbar.

Gylfi Sigurdson dispatched a 75th minute penalty-kick high into the net, but in the 90th minute Ivan Perisic received the ball in the box and fired it past Halldorsson to give Croatia the win.

Group F

Mexican losers celebrate

Sweden 3 Mexico 0 (Ekaterinburg)

Sweden turned the table around with a 3-0 victory over leaders Mexico who also qualify thanks to a gift from South Korea.

A free kick by Berg from the left side of the box in the 5th minute was punched off the line by Ochoa, while at the other end in the 17th minute Vela saw his shot fly inches wide of the upright. Just after the half-hour mark, Berg's outstretched toe-poke was tipped over by the keeper, but in the 50th minute a miskick by Claesson fell to Ludwig Augustinsson who fired past the keeper from the left of the 6-yard box to give Sweden the lead. Ten minutes later Sweden broke through and a mistimed tackle resulted in the referee pointing to the penalty spot from where Andreas Grandqvist picked the top corner.

In the 74th minute, the Swedes went further ahead when a long throw-in was headed on and inadvertently bundled over the line for an own goal. Mexico waited anxiously for news from the other match before they could begin to celebrate with Sweden.

Wednesday June 27th

Group F

South Koreans dump Germany out

South Korea 2 Germany 0 (Kazan)

World champions Germany finished bottom of their group after being humiliated with 2 late goals by South Korea.

In the 19th minute, Neuer failed to hold onto a Wooyoung free kick but knocked the loose ball away and 2 minutes after the break Germany came close but Cho dived brilliantly to his right to save a free header from Kimmich.

With 4 minutes to go, Hummels missed the target with a free header that came off his shoulder and 2 minutes later Kroos scuffed his shot in the box and Cho got down to make an easy save, but 2 minutes into stoppage time the ball from a corner kick was prodded on to Kim Young-gown in front of goal who dispatched it into the roof of the net and after reviewing VAR for a possible offside, the goal was given.

With time running out, the Germans desperately pushed forward and Neuer was dispossessed in the in the Korean half by Sun Jeo who punted the ball upfield for Son Heung-Min to roll into the empty goal and confirm Germany's exit from the World Cup.

Group E

Brazil safe

Brazil 2 Serbia 0 (Moscow)

Serbia were unable to cause an upset as a goal in each half saw Brazil progress into the next round as group winners.

Paulinho latched onto a through ball from Coutinho in the 36the minute and knocked it over Stojkovic to open the scoring for Brazil. In the 61st minute Alisson could only punch Rukavina's low ball onto the stooping head of Mitrovic but his header struck Thiago Silva and 2 minutes later the same player headed down straight at the keeper.

Thiago Silva doubled Brazil's lead in the 68th minute when he headed in a corner at the near post. Stojkovic dived to keep out a thumping shot from Felipe Luis in the 71st minute and in the 86th minute Neymar came face to face with Stojkovic but couldn't knock the ball past his outstretched arms.

In stoppage time Neymar failed to get round the keeper and add to Brazil's tally, but a two-goal win was enough to see Brazil top their group.

Group E

Swiss roll on

Switzerland 2 Costa Rica 2 (Nizhny Novgorod)

Costa Rica scored their first goals and registered a point but Switzerland make it through to the next round.

Sommer got down to make a fantastic fingertip save from a powerful Borges header in the 6th minute and 4 minutes later Colindres hit the underside of the bar with a shot from the edge of the area. However, it was Switzerland who scored first, when a cross from the right was headed back for Blerim Dzemaili to lash in from close range.

Costa Rica equalised in the 56th minute when Kendall Watson rose to head in from a corner. In the 78th minute a header from Drmic hit the top of the upright but in the 87th minute Zakaria from the right found Drmic in the box who found the bottom corner of the net to give Switzerland the lead.

Costa Rica levelled the match in stoppage time when Ruiz's thumping penalty hit the bar and went in off the Swiss keeper.

Thursday June 28th

Group H

Senegal get their cards

Colombia 1 Senegal 0 (Samara)

Colombia are through to the round of 16 after a 1-0 win over Senegal who go out to Japan on the yellow-card rule.

In the 17th minute Mane was through on goal, but Sanchez made a timely tackle in the box which the referee deemed to be a foul but changed his decision after help from VAR. Senegal were the better side in the first half, but Colombia got more into the game after the break and in the 74th minute Yerry Mina's downward header from a corner bounced up and into the roof of the net with Ndiaye unable to keep it out.

Senegal began to push for the equaliser they needed and in the 77th minute Ospina parried an angled shot from Ismaila that was headed away for a corner from which Ospina got down to prevent an own goal from a header. Senegal were unable to get the draw they needed, and the World Cup lost its last representative from Africa.

Group H

Japan rely on fair play

Poland 1 Japan 0 (Volgograd)

Poland left the World Cup with a 1-0 win over Japan that saw the Asian side through having received fewer yellow cards than Senegal.

In the 13th minute Fabianski got down to keep Muto's shot out of the bottom corner while at the other end in the 33rd minute Kawashima made an even more spectacular save when he clawed a Grosicki header off the goal-line. Two minutes later, a low angled shot was parried by the Polish keeper, but in the 59th minute the deadlock was broken when a free kick was floated into the box onto the foot of Jan Bednarek who knocked it in for Poland.

In the 74th minute Lewandowski connected to a pass into the box but scooped it over. Japan go through thanks to their better fair play record, but perhaps their blatant time wasting towards the end of the match will cast a shadow on their reputation.

Group G

England lose momentum

Belgium 1 England 0 (Kaliningrad)

Belgium defeated England to win their group and set up a meeting with Japan in the next round.

Pickford palmed away an awkward shot from Tielemans in the 6th minute and 4 minutes later Cahill cleared off the line when Batshuayi poked the ball from under Pickford.

In the 50th minute Adnan Januzaj teed himself up in the box and curled the ball beautifully past Pickford into the far top corner.

England came closest in the 66th minute when Rashford was clear on goal but he missed his chance and in the 89th minute Pickford dived to punch away a rasping shot from Mertens. England will face Colombia in the next round.

Group G

A matter of pride

Tunisia 2 Panama 1 (Saransk)

Tunisia came from behind to beat Panama and go home with a win under their belt.

Panama celebrated taking the lead in the 33rd minute when a shot from Rodriguez took a deflection and wrong-footed the keeper, but Tunisia drew level in the 51st minute when after some quick passing the ball reached Fakhreddine Ben Youssef who knocked it past the keeper from 6 yards out. Two minutes later, Penedo saved with his foot from Ben Youssef who got into the box after the referee had played advantage following a foul outside the area.

Tunisia got the winner in the 66th minute when Haddadi slipped the ball past the keeper from the edge of the 6-yard box for a Khazri tap in.

Group Tables

and

Knockout Stage

Group A

Pos	Team	Pld	W	D	L	GF	GA	GD	Pts
1	Uruguay	3	3	0	0	5	0	5	9
2	Russia	3	2	0	1	8	4	4	6
3	Saudi Arabia	3	1	0	2	2	7	−5	3
4	Egypt	3	0	0	3	2	6	−4	0

Group B

Pos	Team	Pld	W	D	L	GF	GA	GD	Pts
1	Spain	3	1	2	0	6	5	1	5
2	Portugal	3	1	2	0	5	4	1	5
3	Iran	3	1	1	1	2	2	0	4
4	Morocco	3	0	1	2	2	4	-2	1

Group C

Pos	Team	Pld	W	D	L	GF	GA	GD	Pts
1	France	3	2	1	0	3	1	2	7
2	Denmark	3	1	2	0	2	1	1	5
3	Peru	3	1	0	2	2	2	0	3
4	Australia	3	0	1	2	2	5	−3	1

Group D

Pos	Team	Pld	W	D	L	GF	GA	GD	Pts
1	Croatia	3	3	0	0	7	1	6	9
2	Argentina	3	1	1	1	3	5	-2	4
3	Nigeria	3	1	0	2	3	4	-1	3
4	Iceland	3	0	1	2	2	5	-3	1

Group E

Pos	Team	Pld	W	D	L	GF	GA	GD	Pts
1	Brazil	3	2	1	0	5	1	4	7
2	Switzerland	3	1	2	0	5	4	1	5
3	Serbia	3	1	0	2	2	4	-2	3
4	Costa Rica	3	0	1	2	2	5	-3	1

Group F

Pos	Team	Pld	W	D	L	GF	GA	GD	Pts
1	Sweden	3	2	0	1	5	2	3	6
2	Mexico	3	2	0	1	3	4	-1	6
3	South Korea	3	1	0	2	3	3	0	3
4	Germany	3	1	0	2	2	4	-2	3

Group G

Pos	Team	Pld	W	D	L	GF	GA	GD	Pts
1	Belgium	3	3	0	0	9	2	7	9
2	England	3	2	0	1	8	3	5	6
3	Tunisia	3	1	0	2	5	8	-3	3
4	Panama	3	0	0	3	2	11	-9	0

Group H

Pos	Team	Pld	W	D	L	GF	GA	GD	Pts
1	Colombia	3	2	0	1	5	2	3	6
2	Japan	3	1	1	1	4	4	0	4
3	Senegal	3	1	1	1	4	4	0	4
4	Poland	3	1	0	2	2	5	-3	3

Saturday June 30th

Round of 16

Mbappe double kills off Argentina

France 4 Argentina 3 (Kazan)

Kylian Mbappe scored twice as France came from behind to knock Argentina out of the World Cup in a spectacular match in Kazan.

Mbappe ran 70 yards before being pulled down in the box in the 11th minute and Antoine Griezmann, who had struck the top of the crossbar 2 minutes earlier, converted the spot-kick with a shot down the centre of the goal. Angel di Maria levelled the score with a splendid shot from 30 yards out in the 41st minute and 3 minutes into the second-half Messi turned around in the box and took a shot that was decisively deflected past Lloris by Gabriel Mercado to give Argentina the lead.

France were on level terms in the 56th minute when Benjamin Pavard smacked the ball into the far corner with an unstoppable volley from outside the area and 6 minutes later Mbappe collected the ball in the box, made space and knocked the it past Armani to put France back into the lead.

In the 68th minute, Giroud knocked the ball on to Mbappe in the box and the teenager tucked it in to give France a two-goal cushion.

Argentina pulled a goal back in stoppage time when Messi floated the ball into the box and Aguero headed past Lloris to give the South Americans hope, but it was too late and France advance to the next round.

Saturday June 30th

Round of 16

Cavani sends Portugal packing

Uruguay 2 Portugal 1 (Sochi)

European champions Portugal are out of the World Cup after losing 2-1 to Uruguay with Edinson Cavani scoring both goals for the South Americans before limping off.

In the 7th minute, Suarez whipped the ball into the box and Cavani bravely flung himself to thump it in with his face. Patricio dived to his left to keep out a free kick from Suarez in the 22nd minute, but in the 55th minute a short corner was delivered into the box and headed past Muslera by the unmarked Pepe to give Portugal parity.

In the 62nd minute, Cavani received the ball on the edge of the area and curled it first-time into the far corner beyond the diving Patricio. In the 70th minute, Muslera dropped a cross, but Bernado Silva couldn't find the target and Portugal bow out of the competition.

Round of 16

Spain lose Russian roulette

Russia 1 Spain 1 (Russia win on penalties)
(Moscow)

Hosts Russia are through to the quarter-finals after beating Spain on penalties.

A Spanish free kick crossed into the 6-yard box in the 11th minute went in off a Russian defender who was wrestling Sergio Ramos, but 5 minutes before the break Russia were awarded a penalty for handball and Artem Dzyuba fired home with de Gea going the wrong way. Russia held on in the second half and Akinfeev got down to his right post to keep out a shot from Iniesta in the 85th minute and take the match to extra time.

In the 109th minute, Rodrigo sold his marker a dummy and ran at goal from the right but couldn't beat Akineev with his shot across goal. In the penalty shootout, with the first penalties converted by Iniesta, Smolov, Pique and Ignashevich, Akinfeev saved from Koke and after Golovin, Ramos and Cheryshef had also converted their spot kicks, Aspas fired down the centre and Akinfeev saved with his trailing foot to send Russia through and Spain out against all odds.

Sunday July 1st

Round of 16

Schmeichel can't save Danish bacon

Croatia 1 Denmark 1 (Croatia win on penalties)
(Nizhny Novgorod)

Croatia beat Denmark on penalties despite Kasper Schmeichel saving a penalty in extra time and two in the shootout.

The Danes got off to flying start, when after only a minute, a long throw-in fell to Mathias Jorgensen who stabbed the ball past a crowd of players and in under the keeper, but Croatia hit back 2 minutes later when a clearance in the box hit a Danish player and fell to Mario Mandzukic who buried it past Schmeichel. In the 29th minute, Schmeichel fisted away a shot from Rakitic and kept out the follow up from Rebic at the near post before getting in the way of Perisic causing him to blast the rebound over the bar. In the 42nd minute, Eriksen's innocuous-looking lob shaved the angle of the bar and post and with no clear-cut chances in the second half, extra time was needed. With 5 minutes of extra time remaining, Rebic raced towards goal and rounded the keeper, but with the empty goal at his mercy was brought down by Jorgenesn. Modric stepped up, but Schmeichel dived to his left and smothered his spot kick.

In the penalty shootout Eriksen took the first penalty and hit the post with a slight touch from Subasic while Schmeichel saved from Badelj, and with Kjaer, Kramaric, Krohn-Dheli, and Modric all scoring and Schone and Pivaric having their spot-kicks saved, when Subasic got a leg to Jogensen's penalty, it was left to Rakitic who sent Schmeichel the wrong way and Croatia into the quarter finals to meet hosts Russia.

Round of 16

Brazil march on

Brazil 2 Mexico 0 (Samara)

Two second-half goals for Brazil ended Mexico's dream of reaching the quarter-finals of the World Cup for the first time on foreign soil.

Mexico were lively in the first half and Brazil showed signs of danger while Ochoa stood firm in the Mexico goal spreading himself to block a shot after some dribbling in the box by Neymar in the 25th minute and deflecting away a similar shot by Jesus at his near post 8 minutes later.

In the 48th minute Ochoa got down to push away a shot from Coutinho, but in the 51st minute Neymar backheeled the ball to Willian who bust into the box and delivered the ball into the 6-yard area for a Neymar tap in. Ochoa did well to save a Casemiro snapshot in the 59th minute and 2 minutes later Vela's dipping shot for Mexico was tipped over the bar by Alison.

In the 63rd minute, Willian stung the palms of Ochoa after a stepover in the box, but with 2 minutes left, Neymar ran into the area and toe-poked the ball past the keeper across goal for Roberto Firmino to prod over the line and put the result beyond any doubt.

Round of 16

Late Belgian comeback buries brave Samurais

Belgium 3 Japan 2 (Rostov-on-Don)

Belgium came from 2 goals down to complete their comeback and break Japanese hearts with a stoppage-time winner.

A low cross in the 25th minute found Lukaku in front of goal, but he couldn't find his feet and the chance went begging; and 2 minutes later a powerful shot by Hazard was fisted away by Kawashima, but 3 minutes after the interval, Genki Haraguchi ran onto a through ball and after a shimmy in the box, drove the ball into the far corner.

Belgium responded immediately with Hazard slamming the post from inside the box, but in the 52nd minute Takashi Inui smacked the ball from the edge of the area into the corner of the net past the outstretched frame of Courtois to send the Japanese fans into dreamland. Lukaku missed a close-range header in the 61st minute, but in the 69th minute an attempted clearance lofted into the air was headed back across goal with a looping header by Jan Vertonghen over the despairing Kawashima to give Belgium hope, and 5 minutes later Hazard crossed the ball onto the head of substitute Marouane Fellaini who nodded in to restore parity.

In the 86th minute Kawashima parried a header from Meunier and palmed Lukaku's header over the bar from the follow up, but with the match deep into time added-on, Belgium broke through from defending a corner and de Bruyne raced into the Japanese half to feed Meunier to his right whose pass into the box was left by Lukaku for Nacer Chadli to side-foot past Kawashima with the last kick of the match and send Belgium through at Japan's expense.

Tuesday July 3rd

Round of 16

Switzerland deflected out

Sweden 1 Switzerland 0 (St Petersburg)

Sweden knocked Switzerland out of the World Cup
with a deflected goal in a drab match in St Petersburg.

Sommer, who made a magnificent save from
Berg's awkward bouncing volley in the 28th minute,
was mostly a spectator as Sweden couldn't hit a barn
door with a banjo and in the 41st minute Ekdal
demonstrated this when he met a cross just outside the
6-yard box and sent his side-footed volley high into
the crowd.

In the 66th minute, Emil Forsberg made space with
a shimmy just outside the box for a shot that would
have been an easy save had it not taken a deflection
into the top corner.

A minute into time added-on, Olsen saved a
downward header from Seferovic, but Sweden had the
last chance when Olson ran clear on goal and was
brought down by Lang who was shown a red card.
The referee awarded a penalty, but after reviewing
VAR, gave a free kick from which Toivonen's
powerful shot was straight at the firm fists of Sommer.

Round of 16

England survive Colombia shootout

England 1 Colombia 1 (England win on penalties)
(Moscow - Spartak)

Colombia rescued the match with a last-gasp goal to take England to extra time and penalties, but England prevailed.

In the 54th minute of a niggly encounter, Colombia were punished for holding in the area, and after several minutes of Colombian protestation, Harry Kane converted his spot-kick down the centre.

Three minutes into stoppage time, with England moments away from victory, Uribe hit the ball from 35 yards and Pickford dived high to his left to claw it out of the top corner with his fingertips, but from the ensuing corner-kick Yerri Mina's downward header bounced up into the net and the match went into extra time.

Colombia had a good spell in extra time, but England recovered mentally from conceding so late and substitute Rose came close when his effort across goal was just wide of the post.

Falcoa, Kane, Cuadrado, Rashford and Muriel all converted from the spot, but David Ospina made a great save from Henderson and Uribe struck the underside of the bar for Colombia. Trippier dispatched

the next penalty into the top corner and when Jordan
Pickford dived to his right and lifted a long arm to
save from Bacca, Dier stepped up and put the ball past
Ospina with a low shot to break England's penalty
curse and send them through to the quarter finals.

Friday July 6th

Quarter final

Two goalies apart

France 2 Uruguay 0 (Nizhny Novgorod)

France capped a 2-0 victory over Uruguay thanks to a goalkeeping error after Lloris had kept the French in the game with a magnificent save in the first half.

Mbappe could only head over the bar after finding himself unchallenged in the 15th minute, but in the 40th minute of the match, a free kick by Griezmann was delivered into the box for Raphael Varane to send past Muslera with a glancing header. Four minutes later, Uruguay were almost level, but Lloris dived brilliantly to his right to keep out a header from Caceres.

In the 61st minute, Muslera fumbled an innocuous shot from Anton Griezmann over the line and into the net giving France an unsurmountable two-goal lead and a place in the semi finals.

Friday July 6th

Quarter final

Belgium knock Brazil out

Belgium 2 Brazil 1 (Kazan)

Favourites Brazil are out of the World Cup after losing 2-1 to Belgium.

In the 8th minute a corner was headed on by Miranda to Thiago Silva who could only push it onto the post from close range, but 5 minutes later, a Belgian corner-kick was flicked off the head of Kompany and in off a Brazilian for the opener. Lukaku's powerful run from inside his own half in the 31st minute, resulted in Belgium's second goal when he passed the ball to Kevin de Bruyne who arrowed it into the bottom corner from just outside the area.

In the 36th minute, a free header from Jesus went wide of the post and a minute later Courtois dived to his left to punch away a shot from Coutinho, while in the 41st minute, Alisson palmed a de Bruyne free kick over the bar.

In the 76th minute, Coutinho lifted the ball into the box between two Belgians for Renato Augusto to head past Courtois into the bottom corner moments after coming onto the pitch and give Brazil a lifeline, but Courtois proved to be too big an obstacle for Brazil to beat again and in stoppage time when he got his long arm across to push Neymar's shot out of the top corner their elimination was confirmed.

Saturday July 7th

Quarter final

England head to semi

England 2 Sweden 0 (Samara)

Two headers and some good saves by Jordan Pickford gave England a 2-0 win over Sweden and a place in the World Cup semi finals.

In the 30th minute Harry Maguire lost his marker and rose to score with a powerful header from a corner, and just before the break Sterling received a long ball in the box but hesitated in getting round the keeper and lost his chance. Two minutes after the interval, Pickford dived down brilliantly to punch away a header from Berg, but in the 59th minute Lingard swung the ball in to Dele Alli in space who headed past Olsen, giving England a two-goal cushion.

Three minutes after the goal, Sweden almost reduced the deficit when they played the ball into the box and Berg backheeled to Claesson who picked his spot, but Pickford got down magnificently to save and the rebound was blocked. In the 71st minute, Berg turned in the box but his snapshot was tipped over by Pickford who made England's victory easier than it could have been.

Saturday July 7th

Quarter final

Croatia end Russian fairy tale

Russia 1 Croatia 1 (2-2 a.e.t. Croatia win on penalties)
(Sochi)

Hosts Russia were knocked out of the World Cup, losing to Croatia on penalties.

In the 31st minute, Denis Cheryshef played a one-two with Dzyuba before unleashing a stunning left-footer high into the net to send the home crowd into party mode, but 9 minutes later, the mood was subdued when Mandzukic ran into the box and planted the ball onto the head of Andrej Kramaric who nodded in from the 6-yard line.

On the hour-mark, Perisic took the ball down in the box, but his shot rolled off the inside of the post and across goal and the match headed for extra time.

In the 100th minute, Domagoj Vida's header from a corner-kick bounced past a crowd of players and into the back of the net to give Croatia the lead, but in the 112th minute Subasic held onto a powerful volley from Kuzyaev and 3 minutes later a free kick was delivered onto the head of Mario Fernandes who knocked in the equaliser for Russia to take the game to penalties.

Subasic saved Smolov's poor penalty and Brozovic tucked away his spot-kick to give Croatia the edge, but with Dzagoev sending the keeper the wrong way and Akinfeev getting down to deny Kovacic at the post, the teams were level. Fernandes dragged his penalty wide and with Modric, Ignashevich, Vida and Kuzyaev all scoring, Rakitic sent the keeper the wrong way and ended Russia's participation in the competition.

Tuesday July 10th

Semi final

France edge into final

France 1 Belgium 0 (St Petersburg)

A single goal against Belgium sent France into the Final of the World Cup.

In the first half, both teams had periods of pressure without breaking the deadlock. In the 19th minute, Hazard got into the box from the left and let fly, but his goal-bound shot was headed over to safety. Two minutes later Alderweireld turned in the box and fired a snapshot but Lloris dived brilliantly to make a fingertip save, while at the other end in the 39th minute, Mbappe fed Pavard but Courtois stretched out a long leg to deny him from the edge of the 6-yard box.

In the 51st minute, Samuel Umtiti got onto a corner-kick to head in at the near post and give France the advantage and 5 minutes later Mbappe's delightful backheel on the edge of the box presented Giroud with a chance, but his effort was blocked by a last-ditch tackle. Lloris got down to double-fist Witsel's thunderous shot in the 81st minute and in stoppage time with France attempting to wrap things up Courtois got down to hold onto a shot from Griezmann and in the dying seconds tipped Tolisso's low shot past the post.

Wednesday July 11th

Semi final

Croatian comeback denies England

Croatia 1 England 1 (2-1 a.e.t.) (Moscow)

Croatia reached the final of the World Cup for the first time after defeating England 2-1 in extra-time.

England got off to a perfect start when Kieran Trippier lifted the ball expertly over the wall and past the keeper in the 5th minute and should have doubled their lead after half an hour when Lingard played in Kane who couldn't slide the ball past Subasic and could only hit the post from a yard out when he picked up the rebound on the by-line, but with 22 minutes left, the boot of Ivan Perisic beat an English head to a cross and the score was level.

Four minutes after the goal, Perisic got into the box and struck the post with a shot across goal, but Rebic could only guide the rebound into the grateful arms of Pickford who stood firm in the 83rd minute to block an angled shot from Mandzukic.

Stones saw his header cleared off the live in the 9th minute of extra time and just before the break Pickford acted quickly to deflect a close-range toe-poke from Mandzukic with his knee. In the 109th minute, an attempted clearance was headed back to Mario Mandzukic who beat the keeper with a shot into the far corner to shatter England's dreams and send Croatia to a meeting with France in the final.

Third place

Belgium win Bronze

Belgium 2 England 0 (St Petersburg)

England finished fourth after losing 2-0 to Belgium in St Petersburg.

The Belgians got off the mark after only 4 minutes when Chaldi crossed the ball from the left for Thomas Meunier to knock in from 6 yards out.

England only began to show appetite in the second half and Kane almost connected when Lingard whipped in a cross in the 55th minute, but their best chance came in the 70th minute when Dier dinked the keeper after a one-two with Rashford only to be denied by a last-ditch off the line clearance from Alderweireld.

Belgium counter-attacked with some delightful football that resulted in Meunier's unchallenged volley being saved by the diving Pickford in the 80th minute, but 2 minutes later Eden Hazard got into the box and beat Pickford at the near post to secure Belgium's highest ever finish in the World Cup.

The final

France champions of the world

France 4 Croatia 2 (Moscow)

France lifted the World Cup in Russia after a 4-2 victory over Croatia.

The French took the lead in the 18th minute when a free kick was floated into the box by Griezmann and flicked on by a defensive header for an own goal, but 10 minutes later a Croatian free kick was headed back and eventually fell to Ivan Perisic who knocked the ball into the box and drilled home with a ferocious shot past Lloris. In the 36th minute the referee was alerted to a decision by VAR and after a lengthy delay decided to award France a doubtful penalty for handball which Antoine Griezmann accepted and sent Subasic the wrong way to give France a half-time lead.

Three minutes after the break, Rebic saw his angled shot tipped over by Lloris, but in the 59th minute, Griezmann set up Paul Pogba whose right-footed shot was blocked and he hit the return with his left foot past the unbalanced Subasic to give France some breathing space. France seemed to have put the match to bed in the 65th minute when Kylian Mbappe found a gap and rifled in a low shot from outside the area to become the first teenager since Pele in 1958 to score in the final of a World Cup, but 4 minutes later Lloris couldn't deal with a back pass and Mario Mandzukic took advantage of his sloppiness to give Croatia a glimmer of hope that evaporated with time and the French were crowned world champions.

www.ingramcontent.com/pod-product-compliance
Lightning Source LLC
Chambersburg PA
CBHW071832020426
42331CB00007B/1703